Thomesa speaking at Harvard Club of Boston

Preface

This book is NOT just for the Greatest Generation Senior but also for the Baby Boomer, adult child of the Senior.

Educating the families is KEY to insuring that our seniors are moved with **dignity**, **honor** & **respect** keeping **FUN** and ease in the mix.

This book has NOTHING to do with "Last Will and Testament" but everything to do with ENJOYING life to the fullest, making the "best of the rest" of your life or that of a loved one so that THRIVING not just SURVIVING is the everyday norm!

This book will remind you of the important elements that we all must consider as we age. Included will be the boring, yet, of grave importance (no pun intended) to your own well-being and that of your family members, i.e. the facts, the figures and the legal documents that need to be "in order" so that we can carry on with the more **FUN** aspects of life... LIVING the NEXT chapter of our lives!

Top: *Dad (Thomas), Thomesa & Mom (Fran)...* **Bottom:** *Mom & Dad*

Dedication

To my parents: **Thomas** & **Fran Keegan**

They DANCED. They LAUGHED. They collected STUFF!

(Two out of three of the "DO's" ... not bad!)

To my sons: **Dennis** & **Thomas Lydon**

They LOVE. They LAUGH. They hate STUFF!

(They make a Mama proud!)

To my Grandkids: **Boston, Lily &**

Lola Lydon

They LOVE. They LAUGH. They are working on STUFF!

(Train up a child... Great job boys!)

To my sister and brother-in-law:

Randy & Carol Young

They LOVE. They LAUGH. They recently SMART-SIZED!

(Way to go! Time for "The Best of the Rest".)

Thank you both for taking such good care of our parents!!

I LOVE you all FOREVER & ALWAYS

Thomesa

Acknowledgments

Along my journey family and friends have encouraged me to write a book to help motivate and encourage our seniors to ENJOY life, THRIVE not just SURVIVE and first and foremost, to have **FUN**!

They all know my philosophy on life:
"If it's not **FUN**, I'm DONE!"

"Thank you" for getting me out of my comfort zone and making me sit still long enough to get this on paper.

A very special "Thank You" to my sons, Dennis & Thomas and grandchildren, Boston, Lily and Lola for their continued support and encouragement to share with others how important it is to have a P.L.A.N. (it's like "getting your homework done before you can go out and play." P.L.A.N. first, play later.)

Let's Get This Party Started!

TABLE OF CONTENTS

Chapter 1:

Why I Wrote the Book...

It was late summer, I was hanging by the pool with friends sipping a margarita, having fun when my phone rang. "You have to get to Mom and Dad NOW", my sister, Carol, shouted with such emotion! "Why, what's wrong?", I urgently cried in response. Her voice cracked as she said, "Dad's in the hospital and Mom is home alone." Mom can't be alone! Mom has Alzheimer's!

My parents lived in San Antonio, TX, my sister in Dallas. Tornadoes had closed the airports and it wasn't safe for her to drive. I had to pray that I could catch the next flight out of Phoenix. I don't know if this sounds familiar or has happened to you... YET... but it will.

We all know there are 2 things you can count on in this life, Death & Taxes. However, I believe there is a 3rd and that is getting an URGENT call from a sibling or a family friend saying that you need to get from your town to another town IMMEDIATELY to handle an emergency regarding a parent.

While raging storms continued San Antonio was flooding and the power was out! As darkness set in my Mom was still home alone, frightened and in a panic. Thankfully, I arrived late that evening and the "best of the rest" became my mission for my parents right then and there!

I had packed for a couple of days thinking that all would be back to normal (our normal) quickly. As it turned out, I was with my parents for nearly 3 months. Fortunately, I was able to stay the course with them. As my Dad used to jokingly say, "If you could have kept a man, you wouldn't have to come home and take care of us." (Well, I THINK he was joking but I had been married and divorced twice.) I was not the daughter that took after mom with her self-inflicted duty assignment to continuously wait on her man... well, wait on everybody for that matter. Even before you knew you needed something she was up getting it for you! Although, that was more than likely a generational thing. I think the Air Force lifestyle dictated a bit of that as well or, maybe, it could have just been my dad and what he expected of her! It was simply something I tended to openly rebel about in front of my parents, yet, behind the scenes, I really had the same tendencies as my mom. Children learn what they live, after all.

My Arizona summer attire (2 days' worth) had seen better days by the time the seasons changed while still in Texas. Hopefully, I could hit the Base Exchange and purchase a few things to tide me over. Boy, had I missed the BX after all these years since giving up my dependent ID card. See, there is some good in all things!

For the most part this 3 months was not FUN and was not without grueling mental, physical and emotional pain and agony, not to mention the financial hardships on the entire family.

Recognizing the importance of planning for the later stages of life was a monumental lesson my family learned too late.

Decisions made at this time in life are detrimental to the quality of the next chapter of life and quite frankly deserve more attention. I refer to this time in life as the next "LIVING" chapter of life and encourage all to maintain YOUTHFUL MINDS over AGING MATTERS. This can be achieved with prior P.L.A.N.ning. (When such crucial decisions are made during a crisis, it's as though we are merely putting out the fires and hoping for the best outcome.)

I can't encourage enough for families to adopt the 60/40 rule as a guideline for the perfect time to initiate discussions concerning aging matters. This simply means when parents are in their 60's and adult children are in their 40's... LET THE CONVERSATIONS BEGIN! Disobey this rule at your own peril. It is not a matter of IF parents get older; it is WHEN they get older, what will happen if changes need to be made?

Without a doubt it is one of the most dreaded conversations we could ever want to have but hey, we survived the "Birds and the Bees" conversation in our youth, didn't we? Surely, this one couldn't be anywhere near as bad as that one! (Although, in either conversation it depends on which side you sit.) Nonetheless, it is a MUST, so stop all the FUSS and begin to DISCUSS! It does not matter if you are reading this right now and you are in your 80's. If you have NOT had this talk with your family members or significant people in your life, then... stop what you are doing right NOW. Call them, type or write it down! It's really that important. I may sound a bit bossy and "who am I?" Well, I just happen to be a Baby Boomer that experienced with my family, a full-blown catastrophe, having to navigate the rough waters of a crisis that could have easily been avoided. But NOOOOO... we had to ignore the writing that had been on the walls for years. We simply chose to ignore all the signs, refusing to address my aging parent's need to downsize and move into a safer more social environment. While my heart hurt for their well-being, I did not push the issue. Whenever we did approach the subject matter that concerned us as the adult children both mom and dad would say, "We're fine. Everything is going to be OK!"

When your parents tell you that you simply accept it because you want to and after all, there is always a secure comfort when a parent assures a child that "everything is going to be OK", no matter what your age, right?

Despite my dad's major health issues, he had a great sense of humor and loved comedy. How ironic that "Can we talk?" a simple phrase out of the mouth of the famous comedian, Joan Rivers, whose humor spanned generations, was one of his favorite lines. That line lost its comedic thread when my sister and I knew it was time, more accurately, PAST time to TALK. It was AFTER his massive heart attack and bypass surgeries that he decided to take up racquetball. His attitude was such that he kept moving and shaking with a zest for life. He made a firm believer out of me that ATTITUDE MATTERS and LAUGHTER IS THE BEST MEDICINE. He kept his optimism through laughter and fun stories about his Air Force career and travels, poker games with his buddies and yes, all his racquetball challenges with emphasis on his wins. No amount of humor could sway my dad to "talk" until it became a "NO LAUGHING" matter.

FUN abruptly ended, and a new mission began.

My family made ALL the mistakes and so that you won't have to, I would love to share with you this guideline to *SMART-LIVING for Seniors; How To Make The Best Of The Rest.*

Because of my personal experience with my family I felt that I needed to make a difference in the lives of others, so they could avoid what we lived. I had been a licensed real estate agent for many years and after my family crisis I became a card carrying SRES (Senior Real Estate Specialist). I was already an ASP (who wouldn't want to grow up and be one of those... Accredited Staging Professional), my life as an Air Force Brat (BRAT is really an acronym although many of us brats felt as though we had a reputation to uphold.) taught me how to move around the block or around the world while thinking nothing of the task at hand. Weight limits for household goods had us constantly purging and traveling with the most necessary elements of "stuff". Past experience as a truck driver with UPS and FedEx (that reminds me, I asked my dad one time why he didn't groom me for Tennis or Golf and he simply said, "I bought you a truck when you were 3 years old, just look at you now."...not my idea of grooming, however, I digress) I had a relationship with cardboard and excelled in fast pace "picking it up and putting it down." Image consulting and years of owning my own interior design business rounded out my tool belt for exactly what is necessary (outside "hands-on" personal experience) in my dedicated mission to assist other families in avoiding the agonizing perils, the overwhelming stresses and the financial hardships of "late-in-life" transitions.

Allow me to be your "Life Transition Designer" from consultation to close of escrow.

There is a strategy and it begins with a P.L.A.N.

Turn the page to begin the journey......

Chapter 2:

The P.L.A.N.

"P" - PREPARE IN ADVANCE

"L" - LET EVERYBODY KNOW WHAT YOU WANT

"A"- ACKNOWLEDGE THE SAFETY CONCERNS

"N"- NEVER GIVE UP THAT YOUTHFUL HEART & MIND

~~~~~

Knowledge plays a major role in planning for your future. The information gathered will be extremely important in deciding the options that may be available for you as an individual or a couple should changes need to be made to your current lifestyle due to health reasons or for any life altering circumstance that may occur. There is no discrimination in age when it comes to this factor. Prior knowledge of your financial picture and the living options that you desire are more apt to be fulfilled when you are "prepared in advance."

"P"

PREPARE IN ADVANCE

MEET WITH THE PROFESSIONALS

- Elder Law Attorney

- Financial Advisor

- CPA/Tax Accountant

- Real Estate Specialist

- Senior Move Manager/Professional Organizer

EXPLORE ALL YOUR OPTIONS:

- Financials (Know how and when to access your financial assets to avoid penalties.)

- Basic Property Values (Smart-size your biggest asset.)

- Mortgage (Could a Reverse Mortgage work for you?)

- Insurance Agents (Long Term Care or Otherwise)

- Veterans Administration (should you qualify)

- State agency assistance (should you qualify)

- Family Resources

In my personal as well as my professional experience, THIS one element to a P.L.A.N. can be THE costliest mistake that you or your family can make. Get the FACTS, the FIGURES and the DOCUMENTS that you need BEFORE you need them!

(See Chapter's 6 & 7 for detailed specifics from Elder Law Attorney, Stephanie Bivens and Financial Advisor, Stuart Spivak)

"L"

LET EVERYBODY KNOW WHAT YOU WANT

DON'T EXPECT YOUR FAMILY TO READ YOUR MIND

- Create or imagine your own vision of the life you desire in the next 10, 20 or even 30 years from now.

- Be very specific in documenting, describing and detailing how you see the next chapter of your life. (It is all about YOU… keep that in mind!)

- Make note of any concerns regarding health, finances and safety for overall well-being.

- Secure this information in a location known to those who may need access to it in the future.

Go figure…. We are right back to:

➤ **CAN WE TALK?** (Hence, this must be important, right?)

- Share this information with family members and/or with significant individuals in your life that may be tasked with making decisions for you. (worst case scenario) Don't leave it to chance!

- The dreading of this talk may be for naught as, what if you were all on the same page already? It could turn out to not only be the "easiest" thing you ever did but the "best" thing you ever did. Oh, what a relief! It is easy to create anxiety needlessly. Just talk!

- NOW is the time to meet… Communicate, Communicate, Communicate. (When wearing my real estate hat, it is about "Location, Location, Location" but with my Senior Move Manager hat on… the first and foremost is Communication, Communication, Communication! Location will come later.)

- Practice the 60/40 Rule. When parents are in their 60's and the adult children are in their 40's ... LET THE CONVERSATIONS BEGIN! (Yes, this was mentioned before... for a reason. 😊)

READY, SET, GO!

- Be flexible regarding options and alternatives.

- Be receptive to family members' conversations, ideas and vice versa. (Someone may have one that is new and exciting... AND you may just like it!)

- Set deadlines for any research completion for further discussion.

- Schedule future meetings for updating or reviewing the PLAN. (Life happens you know so always review as needed!)

With a basic game plan in place, adjusting accordingly is a win/win experience for everyone. Sadly, most decisions are made in crisis mode, as I point out repeatedly. (Seven (7) times is a charm to hear or read the same information for retention... we are a couple down now with a few more to go on that point!) 😊

Not knowing what a loved one wants when you are responsible for making decisions for them is a great deal of pressure that could be eliminated. This is not only about where to live. A very critical factor is in having to figure out what to do with the STUFF or which STUFF to move to the new location and which STUFF to discard or distribute and to whom. This is still something that pains me about having to down-size my parents from the larger home into the smaller more manageable space while in crisis mode gone wild. Who was I to decide what they could keep and what needed to go?!! Everyone's STUFF tells "their" story. The very essence of an individual could be at stake. When such moves are made it is important to capture the individual's essence, thru their story items. I believe some of the fear we have as humans and especially when it comes to late-in-life transitions and purging some things through downsizing is the fear of losing our being, our essence, who we are and have worked so hard to become. Although we are

not the sum of our STUFF, communication around the

items of importance and *why* they are important can be

very beneficial for everyone. I strive to impress upon my

clients, as well as you the reader, the importance of NOT

creating a burden-some situation for a loved one tasked

with making such decisions for you. Life and death,

health and well-being decisions are one thing but to

figure out what to do with all YOUR stuff is quite another

while you are still on this earth journey or not. Share

what the disposition should be so that it isn't a guessing

game or a guilt trip in the future.

(Downsizing tips and concerns will be discussed in a later

chapter. Adopting an "on-going" purging process can be

beneficial for everyone. Periodically go through your

stuff and retain what is relevant to your NOW. Discard

or share what no longer serves you.)

"A"

ACKNOWLEDGE THE SAFETY CONCERNS

FALLING IS THE #1 ACCIDENT AMONG SENIORS

- Be aware of falling hazards in the home. (Throw rugs, loose cords, step stools or ladders and clutter create falling hazard conditions.)

- Acknowledge the need for housekeeping, maintenance, landscaping and other type concierge type services (in addition to care giving concerns, if needed) that could create an unsafe situation for the individual if not addressed.

- Address any clutter or disorganization concerns for health and safety well-being. (Hoarding has become an epidemic. Do you have stacks of magazines, newspapers, gift wrap, bags and bows crammed somewhere to the point of overflow without realizing it? (I'm just sayin'! You might want to get out the "hoarder meter" as we all have tendencies toward in some area or another!)

AND DRUM ROLL... THE BIGGEST SAFETY CONCERN OF ALL...

- Set rules, guidelines and COMMITMENTS to be honored and followed by all parties when/if/should a concern arise regarding DRIVING!   STICK TO IT! NO EXCEPTIONS!

(When you consider the risks of losing all that you have financially worked for your entire life because of a fender bender, not to mention if it were a more serious accident that injured or killed you or someone else, would it have been worth it? The answer is more than likely, NO!) Be smart in this regard. That independence you think you are giving up by surrendering your keys could end up costing you everything and then some. Play the big shot. You earned it. Call a driver. Be chauffeured!

(Sidebar story: My sister and I had to finally take Dad's car keys due to his numerous accidents that were becoming more and more serious. He balked and pouted and played favorites pleading his case for a couple of weeks. Then he got quiet. We figured that he finally realized the importance in why we had done that dastardly deed. That he understood it was because we loved him and cared, and he knew it was for the best… but NOOOOOO…………………………………………….

One afternoon I received a call from my Dad and he said, "I bet you'll never guess where I have been?" Not in a million years would I have guessed this one! He smugly said, "You and your sister can keep the keys, I just bought a new car."

I was taught, "Where there is a will, there is a way!" Dad proved it every time.)

Don't let this very important, yet uncomfortable, responsibility become a battleground. Decide how this will be handled sooner than later and STICK TO IT!

Haven't you heard that it's more FUN in the backseat? Come on then, have more FUN! You have earned and deserve the privilege of being driven "door to door!"

"N"

NEVER GIVE UP THAT
YOUTHFUL HEART & MIND

ATTITUDE IS EVERYTHING!

- It's about LIVING life to the full extent of the word... THRIVING not just SURVIVING.

- Shift the perspective in your mind regarding aging. (AGING is not an option; Getting OLD is!)

- Age is just a number... Pick the age you liked the most and maintain YOUTHFUL MINDS over AGING MATTERS! (I use 18... I know I should at least have an age that is legal (although it was a legal age back when I was 18)... but that is what I chose; so what if my kids are more mature I am. (😉))

- It is the next LIVING chapter of YOUR life... embrace it, PLAN the experience and then just hold on for the ride!

This time in life MAY seem as though you are giving up your INDEPENDENCE, but you really are gaining your FREEDOM. You have earned the right to "ring your bell" and allow others to serve you as you have served others throughout your lifetime. Trade in the high maintenance, costly home for the smaller more manageable home that allows you to move about the cabin more freely, travel and enjoy life as you intended it to be!

According to Pew Research, 100 people turn 60 every 13 minutes. Some of those fun loving "kids at heart" SUDDENDLY turn into old fogies! They are weighed down and burdened with chores and clutter, mentally, physically and emotionally.

Don't let that be YOU! Be SMART, free up your responsibilities, downsize your STUFF to what is relevant in your life NOW and be first in line to "Make the Best of the Rest" ... of YOUR life!

It is achieved with a P.L.A.N.

Don't hesitate to call me with any questions, concerns or help if you are ready to lay out your strategic P.L.A.N. (480.375.1974)

Be aware that once your P.L.A.N is in place it can be activated at a moment's notice or laid out in a desired time frame that meets your individual needs and desires as well as adjusted as needed.

When the WORK is DONE; Go have FUN!

The next LIVING chapter of your life is a very important one. Your "essence" is what you bring to this chapter. While many express the fear of change or fear of the unknown, in my experience it seems to be the fear of losing the essence of your being... who you are... that is the most frightening. Consult with those who understand this, and you will be miles ahead of the pack!

I certainly hope you have a P.L.A.N. in place and if you take anything away from this book, I hope it is the desire to create one if you do not. I encourage you to take advantage of my complimentary consultation no matter where you may live. I am in the Phoenix, AZ area but with all the modern technology we are merely a phone call, a face time or a text away! If need be, let me know if I can refer you to someone in your area to assist you.

It is important to educate, equip and empower you as a mature homeowner, buyer, seller or one tasked with the elder care responsibility to successfully navigate the complexities of the next move.

It is my privilege to help you personalize the next LIVING chapter of your life or that of a loved one.

Now let's address:

"3 Mistakes You or Your Parents MUST Avoid When Down-Sizing."

(To be interchanged with *Smart-Sizing* or *FUN-Sizing* from this point forward.)

Chapter 3:

MISTAKES TO AVOID WHEN SMART-SIZING

There comes a time when this dreaded task becomes a must. We all have the instinct of when it is time, yet we tend to ignore that which we don't enjoy. What if I told you there is a way to make downsizing enjoyable, fun and refreshing? Well, there is! I have been known to have had some hair-brained ideas in my lifetime, but this isn't one of them!

First, I encourage you to change the name of the task to SMART-SIZING. We all feel better just saying or reading the word SMART, right?   No one wants to be a DOWNer. Let's eliminate the negativity before it even begins.

Second, I encourage you to AVOID the following 3 mistakes. The **P.L.A.N.** discussed in the previous chapter will help!

1. The "Fortune Cookie" Mistake:

Ah so, Confucius say;

NEVER MOVE WITHOUT PLAN!

We set forth the plan in the previous chapter, so you are already one step ahead of the game. Often, late-in-life moves become the result of a sudden life altering circumstance or a health concern that needs immediate attention. A crisis ensues. This is THE worst time that a move should be taking place. It is not calculated and organized to be in the best interest of the one being moved. It becomes a "hit or miss", "poke & hope" or "this will do" kind of an operation. It can be costly and result in yet another move when conditions or situations improve. Who wants to move TWICE (or even more)? I bet you are not raising your hand right now saying, "I do, I do!" However, that is generally the case when no forethought or **P.L.A.N.** ahead of time has been created.

2. The "Macauley Culkin" Mistake: We all remember the child star in the movie "Home Alone".

NEVER DO IT ALONE!

Growing up may have taken a village! As we age it takes a TEAM.

That TEAM needs to consist of the professionals such as an Elder Law Attorney, Financial Advisor & Wealth Manager, a Concierge Senior Real Estate Specialist (trained in smart-sizing your home) who will refer a Mortgage expert (to evaluate if a Reverse Mortgage is right for you... it is not for everyone), as well as an "Age-In-Place" Designer for possible modifications to a current home or a new, smaller more manageable home or condo. Last but certainly not least, if needed, a Care Management Advisor to insure well-being wherever you may move, and that proper care is managed.

Talking with the professionals allows you to get all the FACTS (options available for individual or specific needs) FIGURES (real estate valuations, personal portfolio of funds available, cost factors of new living space options, organizing, packing and moving expense estimates) and the DOCUMENTS (all legal documents, i.e. Powers of Attorney, Living Trusts or Wills that will be crucial to have in place BEFORE they are needed.)

3. The "Winston Churchill" Mistake: His most famous speech

NEVER, NEVER, NEVER GIVE UP!

Just the thought of this process can stop one in their tracks. It can be mentally, physically and emotionally overwhelming. Where to start? The task seems impossible. It weighs you down and steals your joy just thinking about it. It is very important to never give up that youthful heart and mind! Always maintain "YOUTHFUL MINDS over AGING MATTERS".

Mindset is vital... Never Give Up... Attitude IS Everything!

P.L.A.N. in place, MISTAKES avoided, FUN-Size time!

Chapter 4:

SMART-SIZING/FUN-SIZING

"I have a collection of sea shells. I keep them stored on all the beaches around the world."

Steven Wright, comedian.

A novel idea! But not the case for many of us. Whatever our prized collection (or just our excess STUFF) may be, it is more than likely stored in every nook and cranny imaginable in our households, garages, attics and basements, if we have one, until the entire home is bulging at the seams. Why, then the next thing we red-blooded Americans do is to run down the street and rent one or two of those big metal boxes (called storage units), fill it up and put a pad lock on it. Would you agree?

What is up with that? What are we thinking? Or are we?

It is hard to tidy up *what* you have without thinking about *why* you have it and what you really *want*.

I am no psychologist but there are many studies that encourage us to get in touch with *"why"* we allow clutter into our lives. Physical clutter is emotional clutter. It's displaced attention and deferred decisions. Once we get in touch with our *"why"* then we will get it done. If we improve our environment; we improve our state of mind. It can consume our time and energy. When our lives are filled with more than we can handle, we start "piling on" so to speak. Overwhelm introduced the word clutter.

Webster defines "CLUTTER": {to fill or cover with scattered or disordered things that impede movement or reduce effectiveness; a crowded or confused mass or collection.} And then define "STUFF": {a group or pile of things that are not specifically described; a scattering of miscellaneous objects or articles.} I don't know about you but just by definition those words make my skin itch. Interestingly, neither of them is a sexy word!

For many years I called it "TASTEFUL CLUTTER" to justify it. My Mom, rest her sweet soul, coined that phrase and it felt good because it was so pretty. As I age, youthfully,

I realize that clutter of any kind is very distracting. By clearing away distractions you can enjoy doing the things you love to do for your own pleasure and FUN!

Take your life back!

INDEPENDENCE Day comes when you realize that decluttering and smart-sizing is FREEDOM at its finest.

IMAGINE leaning into INTENTION and releasing RESISTANCE of letting go of stuff! Take the STUFF challenge and see how much FUN you create without even trying.

Depending on the size of the task at hand follow some simple guidelines below to manage more easily if you are taking this own by yourself. Be aware there are many services available for hire for such challenges. Professional Organizers or Senior Move Managers and Concierge Senior Real Estate Specialists can be hired or consulted for help in alleviating some or all of the entire process. You may choose to sit on the sofa or the bedside chair and simply point to the labeled boxes (keep reading) and watch someone else do the heavy lifting.

If you take this on yourself it can be FUN to bring in family members and create your own game of sorts (no pun intended). After all THEY helped in this accumulation. One enjoyable way to play is to have everyone in the household agree to complete a 30-day challenge. On the first day of the month everyone tosses or gives away 1 item. On the second day everyone tosses or gives away 2 items. On the third day everyone tosses or gives away 3 items. You catch the drift! Seems a no-brainer too, right? Until you hit those double digits... ugh.... On day 10 everyone tosses or gives away 10 items as you trek up to day 30 and then 30 (yes, THIRTY) items must be tossed or given away. WHEW! That would be 465 items per person in the household in a 30-day period! GONE! If you live alone invite a friend to play along and let the challenge begin. Rinse and Repeat, Rinse and Repeat until what remains pertains to your life as it is today... not yesterday... not tomorrow... but strictly what is relevant TODAY! Have FUN!

If you are already planning for a smart-sizing move (great idea 😊 by the way) start early. A **minimum** of 90 days is recommended. Just decluttering? Same guidelines below apply.

Once you determine in which location or room you will begin, ring the bell to begin Round 1.

With each item you will need to ask yourself 3 questions when sorting or organizing.

1. Does it have **value**?

2. Does it bring me **joy**?

3. Does it have **purpose**?

Sometimes there is a 4th question if an item is determined to have purpose. Do you have additional items that serve the same purpose? Multiples can be shared with others. If you cannot answer YES to at least ONE of the questions above, then LET IT GO!

Here we go: Let the FUN begin! BREATHE! & AGAIN!

- Clear the clutter in your mind before you begin

- Clear the clutter on your calendar before you schedule sessions (Limit sessions to no more than 3 hours at a time. Sort too long and you will be frustrated and dread the next scheduled session.)

- Select room/location (Begin in the least emotional space 1st.)

- Begin small and move to larger (The same way you would eat the elephant... one bite at a time.)

- Complete each selected room before tackling another

- Complete one closet, one drawer at a time (Experience the feeling of completion to reduce overwhelm.)

- Categorize/color code large item for:

    a.) Sell   b.) Donate   c.) Trash

    (Mark by using colored painter's tape to eliminate adhesive damage to items)

- Label 3 boxes for smaller items:

    a.) Sell   b.) Donate   c.) Trash

- You will NOT need a box labeled MAYBE (Just sayin')

- Bin/Box for anything paper! (Sorting through paper items can be too time consuming to sort as you go. Save for going through when you are watching TV or listening to music.)

- Stay in the room during sorting session (If an item belongs in another room place at the door to distribute later. You know how easy it will be to become distracted and begin working in another location. Consider this a friendly reminder. ☺)

- Apply the OHIO rule (Only Handle It Once)

- Make periodic runs to distribute donated items (This keeps the space clear and allows you to see progress as you go which is a must for your mind chatter)

- Was it a *gift*? If you don't need it. Take a picture! Let it go! The memory is in the person not the item!

There may be large pieces of furniture or accessories that you may be getting rid of but for now color code accordingly and move forward.

Congratulations, once you have completed Round 1, call a friend and go enjoy a treat. Reward yourself!

Round 2 allows you to fine tune and further eliminate unnecessary items. Be aware of your mind shift. What was so difficult to let go of yesterday has become an easier task today. The thrill of giving is very rewarding.

Discarding trash is a feeling of relief. Giving to others is a special feeling of generosity. Sharing while you are still on this earth journey, the special family heirlooms or keepsakes with the most special people in your life is a bonus that allows you the opportunity and pleasure of enjoying them enjoy what has been special to you and that, my friend, is PRICELESS!

This preliminary sorting and organizing is not an easy task but is very crucial to your strategic overall plan for taking back your life, health, and mobility while embracing a more carefree lifestyle producing more energy and vitality.

Be kind to yourself. It isn't funny when you take on all this stuff you allowed to accumulate but don't beat yourself up. It creeps up on everyone just like those skin growths or that excess neck tissue that developed a life of its own while you weren't looking. That wasn't funny either!

Keep up the good work; there is a sweet spot of new found freedoms awaiting you on the other side of this stuff.

(Check out Chapter 12: Are you Curator or a Hoarder? Take the Quiz!)

Chapter 5:

LIVING OPTIONS

Although there are many living options to choose these days, this chapter is merely going to highlight them.

As a Senior Real Estate Specialist, I invite you to travel with me down Lydon Senior Pathways. From consultation to close of escrow my desire is to encourage everyone whose path I cross to make the best living choices for their life no matter their age.

It is, after all, the next LIVING chapter of your life. Make it count!

Many times, the large, high maintenance home is more of a burden on us as we get older. It no longer overflows with joy and vibrance like it did at one time. It has become too much of a work load, a hazard in some respects and costly to maintain. How many of the rooms in your home are now simply storing the Christmas decorations and the extra leaf for the dining room table that is rarely used as well as the bedroom set that hasn't felt the warm body of even the family pet in years.

Property taxes for the extra square footage you no longer need much less utilize except for that STUFF is constantly increasing. Utilities alone just to heat and cool these empty rooms is such a waste of hard earned money. The only time these rooms are frequented is when you must go in to do the regular cleaning. GRRR! MORE WORK and ENERGY DRAIN on you!

Your home expresses how you feel. W.C. Fields once said, "We shape our buildings and then our buildings shape us." How is your home making you feel right now? What kind of shape are you in at the end of each day. Scan your environment and be aware, be very aware. Are you feeling lonely? Has your mood been shaped into something less than joyful? Where is the FUN in this?

There are options to avoid losing your enthusiasm and zest for life.

1. FUN-Size to a smaller more manageable home or condo where you can THRIVE not JUST SURVIVE.

2. Age-In-Place design remodel the smaller home

3. Age Restricted Active Adult Communities

4. Independent Living Communities (Buy-in or lease)

5. Assisted Living Communities

6. Memory Care Communities

7. Co-op Housing

8. Shared housing

9. Move in with friends and share expenses

10. Move in with Family (Nex-Gen home or Casita)

No matter which path you select for your next home a "to scale" floor planning session is required to insure furnishings and accessories selected will fit nicely. This also minimizes excess move and handling expenses.

A Senior Real Estate Specialist can assist in these areas and much more.

The Senior Real Estate Specialist

There are specific realtors who specialize in working with senior clients. It's important for them to understand the fear clients may have and the transition that the client is embarking upon late in life.

A senior real estate specialist is a certified designation (SRES) that is obtained through training and continuing education. There are many elements and aspects that are part of a late-in-life transition. You want to have somebody that understands the perspective of the senior, understands downsizing, understands late-in-life relocation, and can listen to what the seniors' needs are, is compassionate, and is a specialist in relocation at this juncture in life. It is imperative to have someone who can help find the right options for specific living space needs especially when a move is required due to health or mobility challenges. Senior real estate specialists also have more understanding of needs if a senior uses a walker or a wheelchair; showings may require adjustments. Most specifically home specifications to accommodate the senior's needs must be met. Knowledge in Universal Design or Age-in-Place options for the client is important.

Avoiding multiple late-in-life moves is key. Find the best option the first time. I think it's critically important to have a specialist in this field.

When it comes to the sale of a home your specialist can help you assess if your home would generate a higher sale price if elements were updated or if it should be sold as is. Your SRES can help you to prepare your home for sale by increasing the curb appeal as well as staging the interior as needed.

You want to receive the highest price for your home in the least amount of time without wasting time, effort, energy and money. Knowing whether updates are necessary is a key factor.

- Talk to a Senior Real Estate Specialist to insure you have an agent skilled in meeting senior specific needs and requirements when selling or buying a home. Reach out to me if you need a referral for a specialist in your area.

Chapter 6:

LEGAL PREPARDNESS

Being prepared is about considering and planning for all future contingencies to achieve best outcomes. An experienced elder law attorney can help you choose and put into place the best legal tools to achieve your personal goals and objectives. Most people are more familiar with estate planning attorneys. Estate planning is all about using the right legal documents to plan for the most common "what if's" of life, including but not limited to the following:

- Who would be your medical agent and advocate if you were seriously ill and no longer able to make your own medical decisions?
- Who would have authority to handle your financial matters if you were temporarily or permanently incapacitated due to an accident?
- Who will inherit your assets upon death?
- How can you provide for both your surviving spouse and your children from a prior marriage fairly?
- How can you avoid probate after your death?
- How can you avoid paying unnecessary estate tax after your death?

You can prepare for the typical what-ifs through proper estate planning. So, how is an elder law attorney different from an estate planning attorney? Elder law attorneys focus on issues specific to older adults, and have knowledge in many areas of the law, including the following:

- Estate Planning
- Probate and Trust administration
- Medicaid/Medicare/Veterans Aid & Attendance Pension
- Disability
- Long Term Care Planning
- Family Care Giver and Rental Agreements
- Fiduciary Administration
- Guardianship/Conservatorship
- Financial Exploitation
- Asset Protection
- Special Needs Trusts and planning

If you or a family member is in declining health, or simply want to plan ahead, you could use advice of an elder law attorney. The needs of older adults are often different and more specialized that the needs of younger adults. Elder law attorneys do not just handle important financial and estate planning matters addressed above, but also handle the day-to-day issues affecting the actual care of older adults, such as long-term care needs, medical advocacy, and more. Elder law attorneys are equipped to handle the often sensitive emotional and physical needs of older or disabled adults, challenging circumstances, and family dynamics. We often work with other professionals, such as care managers, financial advisors, and medical professionals to ensure clients have information needed to make the best personal, financial, and medical decisions, while taking advantage of the best legal tools and/or government benefits to achieve their goals and objectives.

No estate plan in place? You are not alone; less than half of Americans have any estate planning documents in place. Of those who do, many plans are outdated. If you do not have an estate plan in place, or if yours is outdated (over three years old), you should seek advice of an elder law attorney.

What estate planning documents do you need? Estate planning is all about these critical documents:

1. The Durable Power of Attorney

This document allows someone you appoint to take care of you and your family during life, as opposed to after death, to step in and handle your finances and legal matters either immediately or in the alternative, in the event of your incapacity, whether through illness, dementia, or an accident as you designate. In the absence of a durable power of attorney, family members often must resort to going to court to be appointed conservator. This causes delay and expensive and unnecessary legal fees. It can also cause arguments among family members since you have not chosen who has priority to step in.

2. Health Care Power of Attorney

A health care agent steps in for you to make your health care and personal decisions if or when you become incapacitated. You should have a health care power of attorney in effect to avoid disputes among family regarding who should make your medical decisions if you cannot and provide a clear point of contact for your medical professionals. Without a health care power of attorney, the law provides a surrogate medical decision maker among your family. This may or may not be the persons you would select. There is greater likelihood your family may need to resort to going to court to be appointed guardian due to conflict. As I always say to clients, the lawyer is the only one who looks forward to going to court.

3. Living Will

This medical directive sets forth your wishes concerning medical treatment you would or would not want, specifically for end of life medical treatment. Most people do not want heroic measures to sustain life if there is no hope of recovery. That said, if your wishes are not clearly set forth in writing your family may argue and even litigate your wishes. Think of the well-known Terry Schiavo case. In addition, without a Living Will you may be the recipient of medical treatment you would not want. In short, this document speaks for you when you cannot do so yourself.

3. HIPAA Release

In addition to a health care power of attorney, everyone needs a HIPAA release. The HIPAA law prohibits medical practitioners from releasing your medical information to anyone, even to your spouse, without a release. You may well ask why a heath care proxy isn't sufficient. There are a few answers: First, the health care proxy is "springing" in that it doesn't get activated until or unless the patient is declared incapacitated. Second, while the health care proxy may only name one person at a time, you may well want a much broader group of people to communicate with medical providers, such as spouse and all adult children.

4. Last Will and Testament

Your Will says who will inherit your estate after you die and who will be in charge of marshalling your assets, paying your debts and expenses, and distributing what remains according to your instructions. But there is a catch: although the Will gets all the notoriety the Will only controls the assets that are in your name alone at death and pass through probate transfer. There are many so-called "non-probate" transfers such that what the Will says does not apply in many situations, including: joint accounts that pass to the other joint owners, retirement plans and life insurance policies that go to designated beneficiaries, and property in trust that passes to the beneficiaries named in the trust document. That said, even if you intend for your estate to pass by non-probate transfer a Will can serve as a failsafe in case other means of passing on property fail.

5. Revocable Trust

The documents listed above may be enough, but you may also want a revocable trust, sometimes called a living trust. A trust is a legal construct under which one or more people, the trustees, manage property or investments for the benefit of one or more people, the beneficiaries. In a revocable trust, typically at the start the same person acts as the creator of the trust, will also be trustee and beneficiary. Not much changes in their lives after they set up the trust but upon death the trust avoids probate for all assets owned by the trust. Financial institutions that are resistant to accepting durable powers of attorney appear to be more receptive to working with a successor trustee under a trust agreement. But more importantly, a trust is a terrific tool for intervening in the event of incapacity for the reason only the trustee can manage the assets. In the instance where the original trustor and trustee (e.g., an elderly individual) develops dementia and becomes unable to handle financial matters, the successor trustee may take over (e.g., trusted adult child or other family member) and protect the trust from mismanagement or theft. In addition to probate avoidance and incapacity protection, trusts are flexible in terms of how they are drafted. They can state any number of specifics on who receives property when, for instance, permitting its distribution over time to children and grandchildren. If you have a trust, it is critical that you obtain legal advice regarding titling of accounts and assets, or beneficiary designations to ensure probate avoidance.

Additionally, estate planning extends beyond the legal documents themselves. You also want to organize your financial and medical information in a way so that if those you designate in your estate plan had to step in to manage things for you today, they would have all the necessary information readily available to reduce unnecessary stress, delays, and expense. You also need to understand how all your accounts and assets are owned, and beneficiary designations are set up to ensure this comports with your actual estate plan and review this information periodically.

The common myth is that estate planning is about death. However, most of these documents are more about life and planning for its uncertainties. At a minimum, everyone over the age of 18 should have items listed 1 through 4 above. These documents are necessary, regardless of the size of the estate.

However, as you age, estate planning may not be enough. You should seek to establish a relationship with an experienced elder law attorney. If you are concerned about affording long term care an elder law attorney can counsel you regarding use of public benefits, such as Medicaid long term care or VA Aid & Attendance Pension benefits, to help pay for home health, assisted living, memory care, or skilled nursing. With advance planning, families can often preserve significant assets against the cost of long term care. Even without advanced planning, elder law attorneys help protect assets and streamline eligibility for public benefits, when needed. If the senior family member becomes unable to handle matters for themselves, the elder law attorney often represents the next generation to help them understand the senior's wishes, estate plan, and properly administer the senior's affairs. If the senior is a financial exploitation victim, wastes their own assets, or makes detrimental medical decisions due to incapacity, the elder law attorney can help with court proceedings or other alternatives to protect them.

In short, the elder law attorney helps create the legal documents in advance of need and gives peace of mind to family. In addition, when the "what-ifs" happen the

elder law attorney can then help the client, or their family implement the plan to promote the best outcome for physical and mental health, financial security, social needs, and general well-being of the older adult.
People sometimes believe they cannot afford an attorney. The opposite is true when it comes to issues of aging; the consequences of not working with an experienced elder law attorney is often more costly in terms of time, stress and money. To find an experienced elder law attorney near you, go to www.naela.org, or www.nelf.org.

Author, Stephanie A. Bivens, CELA, Esq., is a Certified Elder Law Attorney by the National Elder Law Foundation, and owner of Bivens and Associates, PLLC located in Scottsdale, Arizona. Ms. Bivens has over 20 years' experience in estate planning, elder law, and special needs planning in Arizona. She is a frequent speaker and author, recognized in the field of elder law. www.bivenslaw.com
Office: 480-922-1010

Chapter 7:

FINANCIAL PREPARDNESS

"People Don't Plan to Fail, They Simply Fail to Plan"

One of our jobs as Financial Advisors is to help our clients get financially organized. This goes well beyond just the management of our clients' portfolios and advising them how to make better decisions with their money.

With a combined 50+ years of experience working primarily with retirees and pre-retirees, here are our Top 10 Things You Need Think About:

1. Everyone needs a Plan: No Plan is a Plan. We call that the "No-Plan Plan" but it is a Plan. We don't suggest this plan. The results are well documented.
2. Simplify your Finances: Having your money spread out in 10 different places and with multiple advisors and multiple institutions often causes more confusion (You should, however, still diversify).
3. Don't assume all Financial Advisors are the same: Many Advisors are good at helping in the "accumulation" stage of planning. Few are versed in the "distribution" phase of retirement income planning. Also, choose a Financial Advisor who is also orchestrating your Estate Planning AND Tax Planning. Make sure you are dealing

with someone that operates under a Fiduciary standard.

4. Estate Planning: Make sure you have updated documents which include a Will and/or Living Trust, Powers of Attorney, Healthcare Directives and a Living Will. If you don't want to be a burden to those yourself I leave behind...this is a necessity.

5. Social Security: Seek advice on choosing the right claiming strategy for your situation. Don't forget to consider your ex-spouses Social Security benefits. Just taking the benefit when it is first available may be a very costly mistake, everyone's situation is different.

6. Beneficiary designations: Make sure you have named both Primary and Contingent Beneficiary designations on all Retirement accounts as well as TOD/POD designations on Bank & Brokerage accounts. Leaving something to "Your Estate" can be very costly and time consuming for your beneficiaries.

7. Healthcare costs: Have you made a Plan for future healthcare expenses including Long Term Care expenses? Remember "No Plan is a Plan" but not necessarily the best plan. Healthcare has become the single biggest concern for retirees when it comes to income planning.

8. Don't fall for scams: Be very careful about phone calls and emails that you receive. If related to finances, think twice about answering any questions or taking action. Cybercrime is rampant.

9. Helping Adult Children: This is a tricky situation. Can you afford to help your children or is there a better solution? Seek advice.
10. Don't underestimate your Life Expectancy: People today are living longer than ever. The fastest growing segment of our population are those over the age of 80. Plan to live to Age 90 or beyond. Will your money last as long as you do? I recently read that the person that will live to 120 years old has already been born.

These 10 areas are a good start and should give you something to think about and consider. Don't be afraid to seek advice and counsel. Find a T.E.A.M. of professionals to surround yourself with. By having this TEAM in place, Together Everyone Achieves More.

www.MeetSpivakFinancial.com
www.SpivakFinancial.com
Author, Stuart J. Spivak, LUTCF Registered Representative
http://www.spivakfinancial.com
P- (480) 556-9931 F- (480) 556-9932
Supervisory Office:
2300 East Katella Avenue, Suite 200
Anaheim, CA 92806
Phone: 714-456-1790
Fax: 714-456-1799

Chapter 8:

ACTIVE AGERS (not Seniors!)

Why Active Agers Need Exercise...

Today 1 in 3 Americans is 50 or older. By 2030, 1 in 5 will be 65 or older, making this the fastest-growing population segment in the world. This has created a tremendous opportunity for the fitness and healthcare industries to step up and address the unique needs of the older adults.

There is a wealth of research attesting to the positive impact regular physical activity has on the prevention and management of chronic disease. It has been shown to reduce the risk of falling and bone fractures as people age; it can help prevent or lessen a variety of physical limitations, stave off depression and improve mental well-being; and it can go a long way in helping older adults maintain their independence and enjoy daily life.

Some ideas and information below will help you get up, get moving and have some fun!

We lose approximately 10% of our balance every decade after 40. This is the major cause of falls. When we balance, we align our body's center of gravity with the earths gravitational field. So, practicing the sustained effort to center and re-center, brings us into balance but also our nerve impulses, thoughts, emotions and very consciousness.

I encourage active-agers to engage in a **Yoga Practice**. Start with a basic Yoga class and remember this is called a practice! Yoga poses will help one to balance, breathe and helps to stimulate the parasympathetic nervous system. This helps to conserve energy as it slows the heart rate, increases intestinal and gland activity and relaxes the muscles in the gastrointestinal tract.

Water Exercise Classes are a great way to assist balance, core, muscle tone and helps proprioception; which are sensory receptors that receive stimuli from within the body, especially one that responds to position and movement. Water Exercise works a multitude of muscles in the body as all the movements in the water are double concentric contractions. Working with the elements of water with music and timing, you engage all components.

Bone Density is another worry with active-agers, but with proper nutrition and weight baring activities this will help to prevent bone fractures.
Some sources of foods that help to keep bones strong: Dairy, milk cheese, green leafy veggies, soy beans, tofu, nuts, bread made with fortified flour and fish where you eat the bones... i.e.: Sardines and pilchards.

All the activities mentioned above, and light resistance training will help with bone density.

<u>Exercise and Brain Function</u>. Aerobic exercise and resistance training are good for the brain. Most cognition studies compare aerobic exercise programs with anaerobic activity, such as stretching. More cardiovascular fitness is generally associated with more cognitive function plus better brain size and structure in cross-sectional studies in older adults. It has also been said that such exercise helps the hormones endorphin and dopamine which are the feel-good hormones.

As we age, we have these daunting concerns, but the overall evidence is clear. Exercise is something we literally must do to live a better and potentially happier life. I encourage you to find a fun and friendly environment 2-3x per week, encompassing all the activities that have been mentioned. You won't regret that you worked out at the end of the day, but you may regret that you didn't.

That's it; be Fit,

Author, Jodi J. Stokes, BS Exercise Science ACE
CEO/Founder of Got Us Fit
Cell: 661-993-3374
Email: Jodi@jodistokes.com
www.jodistokes.com

CHAPTER 9:

THE IMPORTANCE OF ESSENCE IN DESIGN

As you have been reading this book, you have heard Thomesa reference the word **"ESSENCE"**. Many people do not realize what it is that drives them to create an environment that brings pleasure, joy and comfort into their lives. The driving force within all of us is our "senses".

Did you know you that you have **"7 Senses"** that are now commonly recognized not just the **"5"** that most of us grew up being taught? Scientists have identified up to as many as 21 but here is the current established list:

Sight
Hearing
Smell
Taste
Touch
Kinesthetic
Vestibular

As we adjust our living situations in downsizing it is important to be aware of what we need not to forget to bring along with us. However, in some cases, it may be an extreme change if we have always desired something that was missing in our previous living situation! Exactly "how do we do that?" you may be asking yourselves. Let's see if any of these pointers will help you out whether you are transitioning yourself or moving a loved one...

Sight – Are you a morning person? Look for a place with bright morning light to start your day. If you are a slow starter a more dimly lit morning space will help you get out on the right side of the bed! Have a favorite paint color? Maybe a smaller space cannot handle that favorite shade of green that you may love but certainly an accent wall will bring a smile to your face!
Whether you are an art collector or just have a few favorites it can be great fun to find a new way of arranging a gallery wall or finding just the right spot for your favorites!
Lastly, who doesn't enjoy a room with a view?

Hearing – Are you someone who loves dancing the night away with your sound system blaring? Then a smaller freestanding home may be your best bet. If you have a softer approach, then you are ready to have neighbors down the hall. Either way be sure to bring your music along with you to your new space as it can bring you great joy and relaxation.

Smell – Have you been an avid gardener able to pick fresh flowers when in bloom? We have all experienced walking into a room filled with pleasing scents which can take you back to past experiences. In downsizing you may lose some of your ability to have large gardens but now it is possible to create gardens in containers on balconies and patios. Flowers and plants are readily available at your local grocery stores as well to carry home and to bring to a loved one. Open candles may not be allowed in some situations, but spray scents or scented sticks are another way to fill a space with one's favorite scent.

Taste – So you are attached at the hip to that barbecue grill, are you? Here is some great news! Although many condos do not allow grills on the balconies they do create grilling areas convenient to your building. They can be fun gathering spots for neighbors and families as they are sometimes located in the pool areas. Now here is a side benefit of these situations...MAINTENANCE CLEANS THE GRILLS!
Another plus to downsizing is that many of these communities are located near endless fun eateries. Special occasions or just a quick bite to eat can be had many times within walking distance. Not cooking anymore? Then be sure to have a few of your favorite items in stock for that late-night snack or morning coffee. Communities often have small kitchenettes to accommodate light cooking.

Touch – There is great relief in finally cleaning out clothing and linen closets as well as garages and basements! Make your 'must keep' piles to keep such items as your favorite bed sheets and towels to wrap yourselves in morning and night. You know that wonderful feeling of that comfortable robe or easy clothes. Don't forget that 'throw' that not only adds color to your space but that additional warmth when you need it most.

Kinesthetic – This sense relates to sort of a 'sixth sense' about where you are even if you cannot see the space clearly. As you are looking for your new home ask yourself if it is easy to navigate both during the day and the night for that jaunt to the bathroom in the middle of the night. If not is there a way of lighting the path easily and dimly if necessary to avoid accidents.

Vestibular – Do you have a little vertigo or feel ill at ease in a high-rise? Then sky scraper condo living is not for you. If it is severe then you may always want to be on the ground floor. Even floors and stable furniture may make you feel more comfortable so as not to make you feel like your head is spinning. Be sure to have a chair that will allow different sleeping positions for times when you or a loved one may be experiencing dizziness.

Now you are ready to begin your new chapter. The first half of life is collecting, the second part is about unburdening ourselves. Everyone I speak with shares what an enormous relief it is to travel light once again. They feel both physically and mentally lighter!

Happy trails everyone!

Author, Cherie Rosenberg, owner of Cherie Rosenberg, LLC, is a designer in Phoenix, Arizona, with clients based throughout the United States. Her 36 years in the field has gained her experience in both upsizing, downsizing and remodel as well as design work on five assisted living and skilled nursing communities on the East coast. Contact can be made at: cherierosenbergllc@gmail.com Cell: 480 323-6687

Chapter 10

ATTITUDE IS EVERYTHING

Is it possible that, "As we think so we are"? Or put more understandably, "We are what we think". Could our thoughts and our attitudes really be so powerful that they can impact our health, our happiness, our mood and well-being? Can we actually train our brain to make us happier and healthier? These are important questions for us Boomers. As we age, health is more of an issue now than when we were in our twenties. Good health and well-being are important elements of a great retirement.

A week or so ago, while breakfasting in a small coffee shop in Scottsdale, Arizona with a dear septuagenarian friend, I shared my interest in the questions about attitude. She is optimistic, energetic and dynamic, someone who knows everyone and is vitally involved in her community. I asked her the same questions. Pausing to sip her iced tea, she looked up and said that it was interesting that I had asked her those questions and answered my inquiry by sharing a personal experience. She related that some years ago when her businesses were not going as well as she wanted, she began to feel depressed and discouraged. However, not being prone to self-pity she decided to do something to prop up her sagging mood. She began by creating a Gratitude

Journal. Each morning, before moving into her day, she noted three things for which she was grateful. In the evening, before going to bed, she listed three happenings during the day that had brought her joy. As we sat over our breakfast, she continued with her story, "Well that was that. Within a week, I was back on top, feeling gratitude for all that I had". She added, "It also made me aware of small happenings that I would have normally not noticed; spring flowers, the bird songs in my back yard. My blue mood was gone. I found that my attitude had changed. I was happy, grateful, felt restored, and gratitude did it. Both to Dr. Bruce Lipton, a pioneer of epigenetic, and Dr. Ken Hanson, a well-known researcher in the neuroscience of happiness, would agree that my friend had retrained her brain by focusing on gratitude. The research on epigenetic has explored how experiences and/or thoughts can trigger negative or positive chemicals in the body. Going into the blood stream, these chemicals initiate a genetic process that causes changes in DNA. Those changes can either hurt us or help us and can pass to the next generation. The budding work on epigenetics and cancer is finding a connection between an increase in stress harmones and cancer. Keeping a positive attitude reduces stress and the body's production of stress harmones. These research findings indicate that due to brain plasticity, our attitude, our moods, and our behavior are constantly being changed and re-sculpted by what we think and by what we experience. In other words, as we age, a positive stress reducing attitude is one of the best medicines for maintaining good health.

Dr. Ken Hanson, in his book, *Hardwiring Happiness*, indicates that our brains, in times of stress, veers toward negative thinking, much like a car that swerves to one side if not carefully guided by its driver. He describes the brain as being Velcro for negative thinking and Teflon for positive thinking. This survival-based tendency to expect the worse is adaptive if we are worried about being chased by lions, but in times of safety, negative thinking can become a bad habit that is hard to shake. As we get older, we may tend to slide into a joy-stealing routine of seeing the glass half empty rather than half full. One of Dr. Hanson's solution for retraining your brain is to focus on joy filled thoughts and/or memories for twenty seconds, several times a day. In his book, *Hardwiring Happiness*, he advises, "By regularly looking for opportunities to take in the good, you can train your brain to keep aiming you in the direction of positive experiences" (and positive thinking). We live in a busy world where we are bombarded with negative news. As we age, for our health and happiness, it is vitally important that we focus on what is positive in our lives. Remember, what you think changes your neurochemistry for better or for worse. We have a choice. By making a choice to maintain an attitude of gratitude you will be happier and much healthier. There are many strategies we can use to maintain a positive attitude. Keeping a Gratitude Journal, actively validating others, being active and exercising, keeping negative thinking in check by challenging negative thoughts, creating novelty in your life with new experiences, helping others, maintaining loving relationship, cultivating compassion, acceptance, and a non-judgment attitude toward others will all improve your mood and your health. Let happiness become a contagious attitude that you share with others. You will not regret the effort. You and all around you will be happier and healthier.

Author, Gabrielle Lawrence, Ph.D. is a licensed psychologist in private practice in the state of Arizona. She is a clinical member of the American Association of Marriage and Family Therapist, a Registered Play Therapist and Play Therapy Supervisor, and a trauma and loss specialist for children and adults. Dr. Lawrence received her master's in Early Learning and Development in 1973 and her doctorate in Counseling Psychology from Columbia University. In her private practice, she specializes in dealing with PTSD, traumatic loss, bereavement, couples in crisis, parenting, divorce adjustment, children, adolescents and adults with issues of early trauma and abuse.
She regularly lectures and trains locally and nationally for schools, hospitals, professionals in mental health, in corporate and community organizations concerning issues related to traumatic loss, parenting, bereavement, domestic violence, attachment and bonding, child development, couple ship and relationship management topics such as stress management, anger management and conflict resolution.

Chapter 11:

WTF (WOW THAT'S FUN)

We did all the hard work first. Like I said in the beginning of the book; get your homework done first and then you can go out and play. Creating the **P.L.A.N.**, learning the mistakes to avoid, **SMART**-sizing to be **FUN**-sized, learning what living options are available, elder law and financial preparedness, the importance of active aging, designing for the senses and embracing gratitude for attitude will now allow you to chill out and have some **FUN**.

Music, **dancing** and **laughing** are the main ingredients in the recipe for **FUN**!

I think you are aware by now that "If it's not **FUN**, I'm **DONE**" is my motto... Can't think of a better one, can you?

What else can keep you young at heart and help you maintain *"Youthful Minds over Aging Matters"*? Yes, you are right, SEX should be at the top of the list, but since this is a "G" rated book and I am not looking to offend anyone... we will just move right along. Who knows what Vol. II might include. ☺

Until then **SWING YOUNG!**

Below you will find the label of the key ingredients in the **FUN** recipe.   **Practice, Perform, Repeat**

Music: The science or art of ordering tones or sounds in succession, in combinations, and in temporal relationships to produce a composition having unity and continuity.

The BENEFITS of listening to Music:

- Reduces stress and anxiety

- Lifts your mood

- Boosts your health

- Helps you sleep better

- Takes away your pain

- Go figure – Even makes you smarter

Dance: A series of rhythmic and patterned bodily movements usually performed to music.

The BENEFITS of Dancing:

- Making new friends – Social engagement

- Builds self-confidence

- Improves Posture

- Reduces stress

- Helps regulate weight by burning calories

- Increases flexibility

- Builds strong muscle

- Increases coordination

- Increases stamina as it provides routine exercise

- It's **FUN** and keeps you young

Laughter: A cause of merriment.

The BENEFITS of Laughing: It's the BEST Medicine

- Reduces stress

- Boosts the immune system

- Decreases stress hormones

- Increases Infection-fighting antibodies, improving resistance to disease

- Triggers physical & emotional changes in the body

- Diminishes pain

- Strengthens relationships

- Improves emotional health

- Add years to your life

- An antidote to conflict

- Keeps you grounded, focused and alert

- Relaxes the entire body

"I love people who make me laugh. I honestly think it's the thing I like the most – to laugh. It cures a multitude of ills. It is probably the most important thing in a person."   Audrey Hepburn

These 3 powerful elements could be the best "antioxidants" at our disposal.

The warning on the bottle should read:

Take at your own Risk for Improvement; Avoid at your own Peril and Detriment.

Guaranteed to create "Stylish Energy with Positive Excitement, Vigor and Joy. The flow of LIFE ENERGY will have one seeking new adventure with anticipation."

Side Effect: Puts the BOOM back in Baby Boomers!

Growing Older is Mandatory, Growing Up is Optional, Laughing at Yourself is Therapeutic

I decided to wash my car. As I start toward the garage, I notice that there is mail on the hall table. I decided to go through the mail before I wash my car. I lay my car keys down on the table, put the junk mail in the trashcan under the table and notice that the trashcan is full. So, I decided to put the bills back on the table and take out the trash first. But then I think, since I'm going to be near the mailbox when I take out the trash anyway, I may as well pay the bills first.

I take my checkbook off the table and see there is only one check left. My extra checks are in my desk in the study, so I go to my desk where I find a can of soda that I had been drinking. I'm going to look for my checks but first I need to push the soda aside so that I don't accidently knock it over. I see that the soda is getting warm, and I decide I should put it in the refrigerator to keep it cold. As I head toward the kitchen with the soda, a vase of flowers on the counter catches my eye – they need to be watered.

I set the soda down on the counter, and I discover my reading glasses that I've been searching for all morning. I decide I better put them on my desk, but first I'm going to water the flowers. I set the glasses back down on the counter, fill a container with water and suddenly I spot the TV remote. Someone left it on the kitchen table.

I realize that tonight when we go to watch TV, I will be looking for the remote, but I won't remember that it is on the kitchen table, so I decided to put it back in the den where it belongs, but first I'll water the flowers. I splashed some water on the flowers but most of it spills on the floor. So, I set the remote back down on the table, get some towels and wipe up the spills. Then I head down the hall trying to remember what I was planning to do.

At the end of the day: the car isn't washed, the bills aren't paid, there is a warm soda sitting on the counter, the flowers aren't watered, there is still one check in my check book, I can't find the remote, I can't find my glasses, and I don't remember what I did with my car keys. Then I try to figure out why nothing got done today. I'm really baffled because I know I was busy all day long and I'm really tired.

I realize this is a serious problem and I'll try to get some help for it, but first I'll check my email. *(Anonymous)*

If you can relate... No worries... Simply...

Turn up the **MUSIC, DANCE** like nobody is watching and **LAUGH** out loud! It will do the body **AND** the brain good!

Chapter 12:

YOU ONLY LIVE ONCE

Although my Mom taught me a great deal, what stands out the most are these 3 valuable lessons:

1. You only live once

2. You can't take it with you &

3. If you want it, you can have it!

I have always tried to structure my life off that wise advice. Looking back, I can imagine she wondered what she may have done wrong. OK, I can see now that maybe I interpreted them with a bit more spunk and vigor than she had intended, but it was **FUN** and still is! I give much thanks to her for instilling those lessons deep within my soul. They have helped me help myself and others when life happens, when changes must be made, or when I just need a little more YESSSSSS in my path! Looking back, I also realize that my Mom, bless her heart, passed away in 2016 after suffering with Alzheimer's for 14 long brutal years, never actually lived her life practicing those 3 lessons. I believe she longed to be able to live accordingly, yet, did not. One thing was for sure, however, she desired that her children never sat on the sidelines and watched life happen. Her desire was for us to live life to the fullest with no regrets no matter how many years we had on this earth. She had lost siblings at young ages as well as the most tragic thing in her life, losing her son, my brother, when he was only 27 years young. She knew how fragile life was and she handled it with prayer.

Here's to you, Ma, for teaching me to "Make the Best of The Rest" of my life no matter what my age.

Although, I had not intended to add this to the book, as I am writing I feel compelled to share what I wrote a couple of years ago...

I started writing this piece in March 2015 but never finished it. Resuming in November 2016, 2 days after my Mom's last breath inhaled here on earth only to be exhaled as she entered Heaven's door, encouraged me to complete it.
You will see that it is sprinkled in present-tense mixed with past-tense and probably many other grammatically errors. Usually a stickler on incorrect grammar and punctuation, I have to say that, today, I am OK to admit that "It is well with my soul" to just let it be!

"Still Ma... Still Fran..."

What a great clarification to the families of those who's loved one suffer from this cruel disease. The 2014 American independent drama *film* written and directed by Richard Glatzer, *"Still Alice"* has opened discussion and clarification in a wonderful way. My mother, I call her Ma, is in late stages of Alzheimer's.
(UPDATE: Ma passed away November 14, 2016)

I have always known and felt that she IS REALLY STILL THERE... inside, behind glazed eyes...she is "Still Ma" or to the world "Still Fran!"

No, she no longer knows who I am, but I still know who she is! It is difficult to sit before her as she carries on a conversation with me because to her I am simply a stranger that just started chatting with her. Out of courtesy she chats with me.

Although that can be heart-wrenching, I feel so blessed to hear her life stories as she speaks to me... "The Stranger". Stories about her life as a child are so vividly shared and they warm my heart. Her excitement at times is with child-like enthusiasm as she carefully details each story that comes to her mind.

We know that the "old memories" are still very clear to the person afflicted. It makes it that much more important to tune in with my own excitement and enthusiasm as if I am hearing this for the very first time and in some cases I really was hearing it for the first time! Stories and words never shared had such impact on me.

I have learned through the years that "fewer words, more smiles and gentle touches" go a long way in keeping her flow of words, laced with ebbs and flows of enthusiasm as she tells her story.

There are so many things to learn as you step into the "Alzheimer's World." It is extremely important that we DON'T continuously encourage our loved one to step back into "our" world, the one they enjoyed with us for so long. Although heartbreaking to us, it can be even "more" confusing to them. (I encourage families to learn all they can about this disease especially when it comes to the means of communication.

For years I have subscribed to a daily email called *The Alzheimer's Reading Room* that provided great information.)
(bob@alzheimersreadingroom.ccsend.com)

Ma is still Ma! She is just in a different phase of her life as the current or short-term memories fade and the older memories crystalize for her. Honoring each phase became my mission. I would usually ask how old she was when she was telling a story if I could not figure out chronologically within my life span where she was mentally in her story. This was helpful to me as I could pick up the conversation with interjecting what I remembered about that time in life as if we were both there. No matter her age in the story, mine would adjust accordingly! When she shared stories about her youth many years before my birth I would just take it in with joy as I learned more and more about this incredible woman!

She was such a prim and proper lady who always thought before she spoke as she never wanted to hurt someone's feelings. She would figure out a way to say what she felt or say what she thought someone needed to hear in the kindest way! BUT... "Katie Bar the Door" when those filters began disappearing one by one. There was so much laughter at times when she no longer had those filters to run her story through and the BLUNT truth with NO sugar coating just came on out! Loud and Clear and Matter of Fact! Absolutely hilarious at times! I only wish I had written down more of those things she said. One of the most recent comments made, that comes to mind at this moment, was as I sat on her bed at her side during the final days, I said, "Could you scoot over a little?" She simply said with her eyes closed, "I could, but I won't." The sweet little lady that always wanted others to "have more than she had" was NOT moving over to share one inch of her bed! I cracked up and still do when I think of it. Ahhhh, there are so many other great stories I will cherish forever from every stage of her life. Her world "before" me, her world "with me" and her final "Alzheimer's World!"

To the end she was "Still Ma"... "Still Fran..." filtered or unfiltered you felt her genuine love and compassion! People that barely knew her loved her for "whatever reason" or for "whatever she radiated" that drew them into her! She had a way about her! However, those who knew her well will love her forever and always! I am counted among those as a thankful daughter!

There is just something about losing the person who gave me life!

Thank you for allowing me to share! She is a big reason why I do what I do! She loved moving, she loved real estate and all the options, she loved designing, she loved feeding your body and your soul. She "was" and still "is" my inspiration and I am in GRATITUDE for the experiences we shared.

Chapter 13:

ARE YOU A CURATOR OR A HOARDER? TAKE THE QUIZ!

After watching the *Antiques Road Show, Hoarders, or Storage Wars* who knows what to shred, toss or save? Are you burying yourself in junk... or, is that overstuffed room a vault of priceless treasures?

"Are you a HOARDER?" QUIZ *Do you...*

1. Lose important documents in junk mail

2. Waste hours hunting your cell phone, keys, etc.

3. Pray for a Trash Fairy to clear your decks

4. Lock your door and hide from guests

5. Hope for hidden treasures in your trash

If you answer YES to 3 or more questions, you are most likely a hoarder.

How A Hoarder Can Become A CURATOR

Cull your precious objects

Unearth core values; write them down

Reclaim your space, 1 foot at a time

Evaluate standards, enjoy the process

There could be a little bit of that in all of us. Just a simple awareness and some guidelines from Chapter 4 and you will have this problem solved as well.

I have worked with hoarders and they are some of the nicest people in the world. Who knew? There could be a little "sumpen-sumpen" there. No judgement! Using a timer to stay on task is advised. Bring in a 3rd party that will stay the course with you and YOU GOT THIS!

Chapter 14:

Tips for an EXCEPTIONAL Life

** Up Your Attitude

1. Remember... No one is responsible for your happiness but you.

2. Don't let ANYONE steal your JOY.

3. Identify at least "one" thing to be thankful for every day.

4. Act enthusiastic and you will be enthusiastic.

5. No matter how you feel, get up, dress up and show up... with a SMILE.

6. Focus on all the good around you... at every moment.

7. Acknowledge daily accomplishments.

** Live Your Life on Purpose

1. Identify a purpose each morning. Today my purpose is _____.

2. Dream more while you are awake.

3. Set goals for enjoyment as well as work related.

** Keep Things in Perspective

1. See the bright side of a situation; expect change.

2. Don't panic or sweat the small stuff. Will it matter tomorrow or next year or ever?

3. Make peace with your past so it doesn't spoil your present or mess up your future.

4. Don't compare your life to others. You don't know their journey.

5. When you feel down; count your many blessings.

6. Realize life is a school. Lessons learned will last a lifetime.

7. Time heals almost everything. Give TIME some TIME.

** Build Relationships

1. Stay in touch with friends.

2. Call your family often.

3. Make at least 3 people smile every day.

4. Forgive often. Life is too short to hate anyone.

5. Spend more time with people over the age of 70 and under the age of 6. Great perspectives there!

** Take Care of Yourself

1. Take a daily walk with a smile… the ultimate anti-depressant.

2. Always make time for exercise or movement of some kind.

3. Eat breakfast like a king, lunch like a prince and dinner like a pauper.

4. Eat more foods that grow on plants and eat less foods that are manufactured in plants.

5. Drink MORE water!

** Have More Fun (Where have you heard that before?)

1. Play more music, sing along & dance more often.

2. Laugh and smile more.

3. Don't worry about what anyone else thinks.

4. Don't take yourself too seriously, no one else does.

5. Stop waiting for special occasions. Burn those candles, use the fancy china and wear your nicest things. Every day is special.

6. Play more, read more, watch more movies.

7. Clear clutter. Keep the useful, beautiful & joyful.

Chapter 15:

IN CONCLUSION

I hope your journey through this book opens your mind to being proactive in **SMART-LIVING** so that you too can create the life you intend and **"Make the Best of the Rest"** of YOUR life no matter your age.

For the best approach to **SMART-LIVING** we have discussed the major importance of the **P.L.A.N.**

Giving attention to legal & financial preparation, smart-sizing your property for safety and well-being as well as freedom, designing your space while maintaining your true essence, aging-in-place remodel if that is your desire, handling the "stuff" and "clutter" that holds you back and weighs you down are all imperative to a life well lived. However, it is equally as important to give attention to putting gratitude in your attitude, maintaining a healthy lifestyle both physically and emotionally through, exercise, proper sleep, healthy, clean eating, hydration as well as maintaining an active social life through friendships, relationships, music, dance, laughter and proper stimulation for brain health.

When "fun", "excitement", and "adventure" are still in your heart and soul, when you want to keep the "boom" in baby boomer , when "style" and "energy" make you feel "alive", when you choose to "thrive" not just "survive" & "enthusiasm" makes the difference, you will love hanging with Lydon Senior Pathways & Real Estate Concierge to keep energizing your game; keeping joy alive and well.

You have worked hard all your life. Allow the professional to design your Life Transition in style... it will be worth your while.

Be a "Recycled Teenager!"

Go have **FUN** while we get it DONE!

Turn the page to BEGIN the PATH...

Begin the Path to
"Youthful Minds over Aging Matters" now!

LYDON Senior Pathways
Indeed, a guide for future days
Without a direct one to follow
Loved ones for sure will just wallow
In the emotional stress and stain
Going through all the motions in pain.

Having experienced this in my own life
I became determined to alleviate such strife
When a senior needs attention
Families find it hard to mention
As in denial we are best suited
To remain in the lifestyle we are rooted.

To make a move or a change
Oh no, there is too much to re-arrange
Aging while remaining upbeat
May be the most difficult part of the feat.

Senior Transitions, a new phrase
Yes, seek assistance for those coming days
Can't erase it from being
Might I suggest you start seeing
What LYDON Senior Pathways suggests
As it will all be for your best.

A consultation with one and all
Making a P.L.A.N. to kick-start that ball
Getting it rolling in the right direction
Eliminating need for any correction.

By planning, organizing and such
Allowing LYDON Senior Pathway's magical touch
To manage the entire transition
Brings peace of mind to all involved on this mission,
Seniors and Baby Boomers need only set the date
It even includes staging and selling of your real estate.

Experience no worry and no hassle
As off you go to your next awaiting castle.
Your anxiety and fear now shatters
As you fully embrace "Youthful Minds over Aging Matters!"

By: Thomesa Lydon

RESOURCES

Legal Preparedness:

Stephanie A. Bivens, *CELA, Esq.,* is a Certified Elder Law Attorney by the National Elder Law Foundation, and owner of Bivens and Associates, PLLC located in Scottsdale, Arizona. Ms. Bivens has over 20 years' experience in estate planning, elder law, and special needs planning in Arizona. She is a frequent speaker and author, recognized in the field of elder law. www.bivenslaw.com 480 922-1010

Financial Preparedness:

Stuart J. Spivak, LUTCF Registered Representative, is a Financial Planner with more than 30 years of wisdom, knowledge and experience in the financial services industry. A 1987 graduate of Pennsylvania State University (Penn State), he also holds many professional certifications and licenses as a financial professional, including the Series 7 and Series 65 Securities Licenses. His extensive background in Tax and Estate Planning and focus on Wealth Preservation and Retirement Safety allow him to provide a wide array of financial services to his clients.
www.MeetSpivakFinancial.com
www.SpivakFinancial.com
http://www.spivakfinancial.com
P- (480) 556-9931 F- (480) 556-9932
Supervisory Office:
2300 East Katella Avenue, Suite 200
Anaheim, CA 92806
Phone: 714-456-1790
Fax: 714-456-1799

Active Agers (Health & Fitness)

Jodi J. Stokes, BS Exercise Science ACE, has 30+ years of experience and success in creating personal fitness plans through analyzing YOUR body. Plans include healthy eating, exercise and behavior modifications to ensure obtaining life-changing results.
Cell: 661 993-3374
www.jodistokes.com
Jodi@jodistokes.com

RESOURCES

The Importance of Essence in Design

Cherie Rosenberg, owner of Cherie Rosenberg, LLC, is a designer in Phoenix, Arizona with clients based throughout the United States. Her 36 years in the field has gained her experience in both upsizing and downsizing, remodeling as well as working on five assisted living and skilled nursing communities on the East Coast.
cherierosenbergllc@gmail.com
Cell: 480 323-6687

Attitude is Everything

Gabrielle Lawrence, Ph.D. is a licensed psychologist in private practice in the state of Arizona. She is a clinical member of the American Association of Marriage and Family Therapist, a Registered Play Therapist and Play Therapy Supervisor, and a trauma and loss specialist for children and adults. Dr. Lawrence received her master's in Early Learning and Development in 1973 and her doctorate in Counseling Psychology from Columbia University. In her private practice, she specializes in dealing with PTSD, traumatic loss, bereavement, couples in crisis, parenting, divorce adjustment, children, adolescents and adults with issues of early trauma and abuse.
She regularly lectures and trains locally and nationally for schools, hospitals, professionals in mental health, in corporate and community organizations concerning issues related to traumatic loss, parenting, bereavement, domestic violence, attachment and bonding, child development, couple ship and relationship management topics such as stress management, anger management and conflict resolution.

Area Agency on Aging (State specific)
National association of Area Agencies on Aging at **https://www.n4a.org/**

Veterans Affairs
1-800-872-1000

Randy & Carol Young, USAF, Ret. have provided valuable resource information for families when going through the process (living or deceased) with a Veteran family member. It can be found on my website: www. LydonSeniorPathways.com (Thank you for your service and contribution to this book and information for the website)

ABOUT THE AUTHOR

THOMESA LYDON, author of *SMART-LIVING for Seniors: How to Make the Best of the Rest,* is a Concierge REALTOR® with RE/MAX Excalibur, in Scottsdale, AZ. & founder of Lydon Senior Pathways.

A frequent speaker on Senior Real Estate & Relocation at NASDAQ, Harvard Club of Boston and on ABC NBC CBS & FOX TV News & Talk Shows, Lydon, a Senior Real Estate Specialist (SRES) and down-sizing expert provides comprehensive one-stop relocation planning, move management, and real estate services, specializing in listing, selling, and the purchasing of properties for seniors in the process of down-sizing (SMART-sizing) to enjoy the next "living" chapter of life.

Thomesa Lydon, SRES, ASP, Speaker, Author, Baby Boomer

Cell: 480.375.1974
Email: tlydon@lydonforhome.com
Website: www.LydonSeniorPathways.com

Let's connect on:
Facebook
LinkedIn
Instagram
Twitter

I am honored and privileged to have Frank Shankwitz,
Founder of Make A Wish Foundation, on my Board of
Advisors.

Thank you, Frank, for all you have done and are doing to
make a difference in this world. Your book was a hit and
I now look forward to the release of the movie,
WISHMAN.

It is also my honor and privilege to have Scott Page, Saxophonist, Pink Floyd, as part of Lydon Senior Pathways' Board of Advisors. Thank you for the joy in music you have and are still bringing to so many.

Made in the USA
San Bernardino, CA
31 July 2018